How to
be fine about
LIVING
WITH YOUR
PARENTS

ICE HOUSE BOOKS

Published by Ice House Books

Copyright © 2020 Ice House Books

Illustrated and designed by Kayleigh Hudson
Written and compiled by Rebecca Du Pontet & Zulekhá Afzal

Ice House Books is an imprint of Half Moon Bay Limited
The Ice House, 124 Walcot Street, Bath, BA1 5BG
www.icehousebooks.co.uk

ISBN 978-1-912867-76-9

Printed in China

TO:

FROM:

Welcome to living with your

PARENTS!

Where you won't shut up about being an

INDEPENDENT ADULT

but you kinda want to be a big kid too.

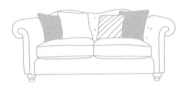

Yes, I would quite like to have
my own house at this point in life.

THANKS FOR ASKING.

I'm an adult and still think of my
future like, "when I grow up".

I would storm out of here right now!

(... if I had some money or a place to go.)

PERKS OF LIVING WITH YOUR PARENTS

Your savings account
(ahem, piggy bank) looks a lot healthier.

The laundry fairy visits every now and then - and your whites don't turn grey!

There's always food in the house and hopefully tasty meals on offer too.

When you're sick there's someone there who actually cares if you *LIVE OR DIE.*

They're not flatmates - no notes about stealing the last bit of cheese here!

I've thought long and hard, but I just don't think this whole being an independent adult thing is going to work for me.

#sorrynotsorry

The wise man and the tortoise
travel but never leave their home.

Chinese Proverb

Turns out my parents don't think it's appropriate for me to build forts in the living room anymore.

I thought it would
be a good idea to write a
contract for my parents now
I'm living back at home ...

PARENT CONTRACT

I promise to ...

Not open your bedroom door
at random times without knocking.

Never vacuum while you're sleeping.

Let you lounge around and not
constantly pester you about
clearing up after yourself.

Stop asking how your 'career' is going.

Refrain from trying to set you up with
every ~~eligible~~ human out there.

Signature ....

Me in my teens:

I can't wait to be an adult and
make my own decisions.

Me in my 30s:

No, but seriously,
WTF SHOULD I DO?

IT IS NOT IN THE STARS TO HOLD OUR DESTINY BUT IN OURSELVES.

William Shakespeare
Julius Caesar

All my friends are getting engaged and
having kids and I'm just over here like …

*Dad, what's
for dinner?*

Respect your parents.
They got through a lot of
life without Google.

I'm doing my parents
a favour by living
with them.

I wouldn't want them to
miss me too much.

There is nothing like staying
at home for real comfort.

Jane Austen
Emma

Funny how my parents didn't want me to leave home, but now that I'm back they're trying to kick me out ...

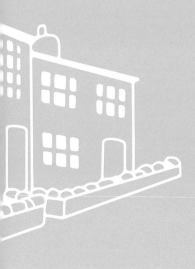

I can't move in with my parents —
my grandparents haven't got
room for anyone else.

Sex on the Beach
Serves 1 | Prep 5 minutes

Ingredients

1 shot vodka
1 shot rum
1 shot peach schnapps
1 shot orange juice
1 shot cranberry juice

Method

- Add all ingredients to a shaker filled with ice.

- Shake to combine and pour into glass.

- Allow your stress to dissipate.

Mum

Hi Mum,
Just wondering if it's absolutely necessary to bash the vacuum cleaner repeatedly against my door first thing in the morning??

...

How lucky I am to have something that makes saying goodbye so hard.

A. A. Milne
Winnie the Pooh

Why did I ever think being an adult would be fun?

Someone show me the unsubscribe button.

Don't mind me,
I'm just wandering around
like I know what I'm doing ...

My parents keep changing the
lock on the front door ...

... rude!

QUESTIONS I CHOOSE TO IGNORE ...

"So, you're not doing anything today?"

"What time will you be back?"

"Maybe you could think about tidying your room today?"

"I think we should talk about your job situation, don't you?"

"Isn't it time you moved out?"

FOOD
MACHINE

Sorry to my parents who

thought they were free of me

when I turned 18.

• • • • • • • • • • • • • • • • • • • •

That's what children are for —
that their parents may not be bored.

Ivan Turgenev
Diary of a Superfluous Man

• • • • • • • • • • • • • • • • • • • •

Dad said "you treat this place like a hotel".

He'll regret that when I give him a low score on TripAdvisor.

How come when I call my parents and they don't answer it's fine, but when they call me and I don't answer, it's like a

NATIONAL EMERGENCY.

#doublestandards

Where we love is home,
home that our feet
may leave, but
not our hearts.

Oliver Wendell Holmes Sr.

I'm going home to a

• •

COOKED MEAL,

WARM HOUSE

AND FRESH SHEETS.

WBU?

The sun at home warms better
than the sun elsewhere.

Albanian Proverb

**AFTER A GOOD DINNER
ONE CAN FORGIVE ANYBODY,
EVEN ONE'S OWN RELATIVES.**

Oscar Wilde

*30 years' old
and living with
my parents ...
#goals*

RETIRED PARENT:

"What are you doing tomorrow?"

ME:

"Work, Mum."

You are going to miss this someday.

... I say to myself, as I realise Mum has rearranged my underwear drawer *AGAIN.*

*When a couple of weeks
at the 'rents turns into
a couple of years ...*

Don't beat yourself up –
it happens to the best of us.

Make the most of your nearest
and dearests' wisdom and
support while it's on tap.

It's not your fault that affording
somewhere on your own requires
the bank balance of a city banker.

Make a **PLAN.**

Save, save, save!

SNEAKING
the new thing I
bought that I

SHOULDN'T
have bought
that my parents

CAN'T KNOW
I bought into the house
because I'm a respectable adult.

FAMILY

A little bit of
crazy.

A lot of
noise.

And heaps of
*unconditional
LOVE.*

When I was a kid
my parents moved a lot,

but I always found them.

Rodney Dangerfield

Deep breaths.

Hold on tight.

Work hard, play a little,
save like f**k and above all,
DON'T GIVE UP ON YOUR DREAMS.

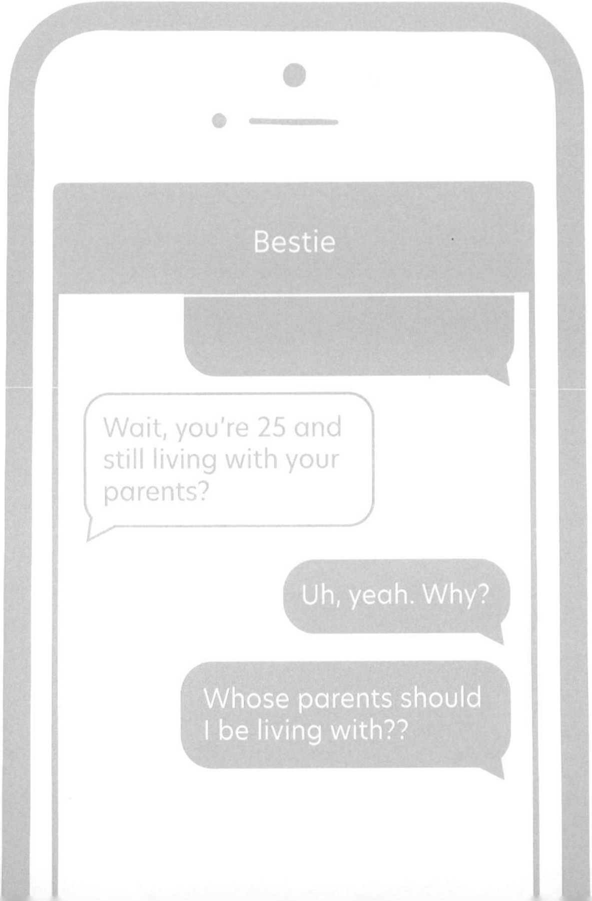
Bestie
Wait, you're 25 and still living with your parents?
Uh, yeah. Why?
Whose parents should I be living with??

To maintain a joyful
family requires much from
both the parents and the
children. Each member of
the family has to become,
in a special way, the
servant of the others.

Pope John Paul II

People keep saying

"YOU DO YOU"

---

but then they're all up in my
personal space like,

"when are you buying a house?"

"when are you getting married?"

"when are you having kids?"

When I'm ready, that's when!

You'll always be the baby whose nappy they changed.

Cut your parents some slack ...

... they've put up with your sh*t for years.

Home is where one starts from.

T.S. Eliot

£1 into the jar every time ...

- A parent falls asleep on the sofa.
- There's an argument over chores.
- There's a dinner-time debate.
- You used the last teabag.

£5 into the jar every time ...

- You drunkenly wake everyone up.
- You sneak in an overnight date.
- You take the family car without asking.
- You book a holiday on their credit card.

Families are like
tree branches.
They grow in
different directions
and sometimes snap.

Remember when you thought people in their 20s were adults?

Now you're in your 20s, still living at home, and eating dinner with your parents.

WTF happened?

I know money doesn't grow on trees.

That's why I'm asking you for some.

When you're safe at home
you wish you were having

AN ADVENTURE.

When you're having an
adventure you wish you were

SAFE AT HOME.

Thorton Wilder

Mid pleasures and palaces
though may we roam,
be it ever so humble,
there's no place like home.

John Howard Payne
Home! Sweet Home!

I don't think it's appropriate
for me to live on my own until
I can keep a plant alive.

PARENTS ON HOLIDAY?

It's time to have some friends round like a normal adult, but still feel like you're having a secret teenage party.

This whole 'working-for-a-living, paying-your-own-bills, making-your-own-decisions' thing goes on for how long?

Parents can only give
good advice
or put them on the
right paths,
but the final
forming
of a person's
character lies in their
own hands.

Anne Frank

Dreams don't work
unless you do.

When all we want
to do is buy our own
house, we forget we
already have a home.

Adulthood is like looking both ways before you cross the street and then getting hit by an aeroplane.

Eventually you'll end up

where you need to be,

with who you're

meant to be with,

and doing what you

should be doing.

Well, hopefully ...

Luckily I live with my
parents and they can do the
adult-ing thing for me.

FAMILY VACATION

• •

A time for you to remember why
your family never spends longer than

24 HOURS
TOGETHER.

• •

When I come home to

smiling faces,

food and wine,

I think to myself,

this really isn't so bad.

My favourite childhood
memory is not paying rent.

Dear Parents,

Thank you for ...

- Understanding me.

- Accepting me even when I royally f**k up.

- Paying off that loan I hoped would go away all by itself.

Your loving child x

Home is the nicest word there is.

Laura Ingalls Wilder

Having an argument
with my parents is like
getting arrested ...

• • • • • • • • • • • • • • • • • •

... *everything I have ever
said or done **can and will**
be held against me.*

The most important
thing that parents can
teach their children
is how to get
along without them.

Frank A. Clark

I don't run away from my problems. I lie on my parents' sofa, eat all their food, play on my phone and ignore them.

BONDING ACTIVITIES FOR YOU AND YOUR PARENTS

Actually spend some quality time at home together - you might enjoy it.

Head out into nature for a hike - great for reconnecting.

Revisit your childhood with an old board game or photo album.

Cook them a meal (or order in if it's safer that way).

If all else fails, treat your parents to a day out so you get the house to yourself.

Me in my teens:

I can't wait to move out of this house!
SLAMS DOOR

Me in my 30s:

What do you mean, you want to use
my bedroom as an ART STUDIO?!

90%

of being an adult is
wondering when you can

nap again.

It's so great living at home again and having my parents use something I did as a 10-year-old against me.

Childhood is like being drunk.
Everyone remembers what you did.

Except you.

When you feel like
NOTHING is going right
and you don't know
what to do next,
drink some coffee
and pretend you know
what you're doing.

Mum
Mum,
would you mind putting some clothes on when you go to the loo in the middle of the night?
Thanks!

The longer you stay the harder it is to

MOVE OUT

(and you can never go without
leaving a load of cr*p behind in
your bedroom, just so they don't
forget all about you ...)

When you want to *SCREAM*

because you can't get a

moment to *YOURSELF* and you

keep *BEING TOLD* what to do,

ALL THE TIME,

remember how lucky you are to still

have a place to call **HOME.**

Sometimes, happiness is finding
the key to the right home.

HOME IS WHERE THE ♥ IS

I'm never leaving.
Ever.

And then comes

FOMO

(Fear Of Moving Out)

● ● ● ● ● ● ● ● ● ● ● ● ● ● ● ● ● ● ●

The cold dawn of realisation
that maybe it's not SO bad
living back at home after all ...

Here's to pretending
that you just got up
for breakfast when
you just got in from
an all-nighter.

(btw, they know)

*A chaque oiseau,
son nid est beau.*

*(To every bird, its own
nest is beautiful.)*

French Proverb

Living at home with my
parents is my way of saving
up to be a millionaire.

One day you'll

miss being questioned

like a TEENAGER when

you get in from a full day

of being an ADULT.

Make the most of living with your

PARENTS.

• • • • • • • • • • • • • • • • • • • •

It won't last forever.